To my family, and to those who look for the good in others, who truly look upon the heart.
You are my people.

-Rebecca Atanassova

POPSICLE
PUBLISHING

P.O. Box 2588 Alexandria, VA 22301
www.popsiclepublishing.com
Copyright @ 2023 Rebecca Atanassova
All rights reserved.
ISBN 978-1-960746-23-8

To tell you there's a certain size,
To the human heart.

Each heart is not the same inside.
It can be bigger or smaller,
And it all depends on you.

I know how it all works.
The key to hearts is this:

Scientists do tests,
To tell if something's true.

Your heart is bigger than the universe!

I know the good deeds that you do,
You're always there,
When someone needs you.

Even on the grayest days,
Shining brighter than the sun.

When they need a friend to talk to,
You listen and understand.

When things aren't working out,
You're the first one to be fair.

You go out of your way,
When someone's feeling down,

To make them feel special,
And turn their day around.

When you see trash on the ground,
You stop to throw it all away.

You make them oh *so* special,
In a million different ways.

I've performed this scientific test,
If I may be so bold.

Your heart is bigger than the universe!
And it has room to spare.

You try to show, in every way,
The whole world that you care.

Made in the USA
Middletown, DE
10 November 2023

42317969R00024